The
Making
Of A
Leader
(ON THE JOB TRAINING)

LENORA TURNER

authorHOUSE

AuthorHouse™
1663 Liberty Drive
Bloomington, IN 47403
www.authorhouse.com
Phone: 1 (800) 839-8640

Published by AuthorHouse 12/17/2019

ISBN: 978-1-7283-4005-0 (sc)
ISBN: 978-1-7283-4012-8 (e)

Library of Congress Control Number: 2019920751

Print information available on the last page.

Any people depicted in stock imagery provided by Getty Images are models,
and such images are being used for illustrative purposes only.
Certain stock imagery © *Getty Images.*

This book is printed on acid-free paper.

Scripture quotations marked KJV are from the Holy Bible, King James Version
(Authorized Version). First published in 1611. Quoted from the KJV Classic
Reference Bible, Copyright © *1983 by The Zondervan Corporation.*

To My Family

My first ministry

C O N T E N T S

ACKNOWLEDGMENT

First thanking God Almighty for from the beginning had this in mind for me to do and with the unction of the Holy Spirit and the word in me to yield my flesh for the duration of time that this book was birth. To my family that without them I would not even have another reason to do it. To show them that no matter what it is God wants to get the glory out of your life. Whether its singing, being a builder of homes, to be a wife, a friend, a husband, whatever God has placed you here to do, do it as unto the Lord and you will be living out your purpose. To a few of the spiritual leaders in one part of my life, Apostle Curtis L. Magazine and Evangelist Patricia Magazine, I am truly grateful for what God has allowed me to learn and be taught by you. To (Lucy) (lol), Danette Marie Ellis Harris. She is the epitome of a soul that has been won. For with the love of God I saw her grow more and more which encouraged me to know that the life that I was living that in spite of what she was going through it did not discourage her to continue seeking the Masters Face. To the ones that I have not mentioned just know that God knows who you are and what you have done to attribute to this book. And it is Him that will give you your reward. God bless you and thank you one and all.

PREFACE

Oh, what a journey that lies ahead. The expectancy of it cannot be put into words. All I know is that **"God Is"**.

I can only imagine how Moses felt when the Lord God Almighty, **I AM that I AM** called him to come near to him. **(Exodus 3:4, 5)**

A leader of God cannot lead except he or she has had an encounter with God to actually know the plans of God that he has for his people.

Yes, God does have a call, a work for everyone to do. But to actually lead Gods people as Moses had being a deliverer is something different altogether.

Just as Pharaoh, the grasp of the enemy with whatever bondages, hindering, fears, esteem issues, that hold people, he does not want to let them go.

As Pharaoh in the beginning it looks as though the enemy has let them go, and is in agreement with what they have confessed with their mouth and believed in their heart, to come away from their past, and start fresh. But we as leaders are to prepare people to know that the enemy is a liar. Just as Pharaoh had agreed with Moses in his presence but as soon as Moses left, he changed his mind. With all that God warned Pharaoh but he did not take heed. The enemy will pursue you for his desire is that you not live a free, abundant and fruitful life here make heaven your home, or show the spirit of God in your life that others may want to follow you as you follow God.

But they need to believe that as they continue to run to the Lord their God and not look back but look to their future and the promises that God has said for them. As God had promised the Israelites so shall that promise be unto them. They shall see that enemy no more. (**Exodus 14:13**)

C H A P T E R   1

Hindsight

THERE WAS SOMETHING ABOUT SEEING A BUSH IN THE MIST OF fire and not being consumed.

Just look at from the beginning how God was showing Moses how the Holy Spirit was going to be in us.

Our outward appearance is the same. Moses recognized the bush, but he also saw the fire.

Yes, God wants us to change but not who we are he just wants us not to do the things that would keep Him from being seen by others when they see us. Moses saw the bush as well as the fire.

As a leader we are to be able to allow the people we lead to see that we are human not a God but yet they have to also see the God in our lives that we say we are following. Remember Moses saw the bush as well as the fire.

God had prepared Moses to come into the world to be kept

alive by the very enemy that God was going to send him back to in order to deliver God's people. How ironic. God caught Moses attention just to let him know that where he was is not where he was going to stay. Don't get comfortable where you are for there is so much more to you than you know.

Where Moses had been living was because he had to escape. He had seen how the Egyptians were treating the Israelites and it went into his heart that he took matters into his own hands and killed an Egyptian. So when God began to tell Moses about how he had heard the cries of his people and saw the affliction and the oppression that the Egyptians were pressing upon them Moses already had the heart to want to help them he just didn't know how, God then told Moses **"Come" (Exodus 3:10).** There was another man that God called to be a leader his name was Peter (**Matthew 14:28, 29**). It is something when you tell God about what you're not able to do and it is then He tells us to **"Come"** as to say to us don't worry about it I got you. We as leaders have to let God have his way for without Him we will not be able to do what it is he has called us to do.

But just like Moses and Peter we still have our doubts about why God would call us let alone want to use us. But let me reassure you God is not concern about what you are able to do He just wants you to let Him do what he said he would do, availability not ability that is what he wants.

We have to stop changing the message that has been established from the beginning from God to man, and that is the message that God has given man a way back to Him to have the relationship that once was in the Garden of Eden. The promise that He made with Abraham, Isaac and Jacob it still applies to this day. That if we would allow Him to be our God to trust and believe in Him, we would be his people and he would be for us whatever we needed... a provider, a keeper, a protector, a promoter, peace, a shelter, a guide, a healer, a way maker...water when we would be thirsty....bread when we would be hungry....

God promises that when he calls us to do anything for Him he has already prepared the hearts of people as well as the way being made for all that He is calling you to do to come to pass.

He told Moses everything that was about to take place when he would send him back to Egypt to deliver God's people out of the bondage of Pharaohs grips. He let him know that Pharaoh was not going to let the people go just on Moses words but that God himself would have to lay His hand on the Egyptians in order for them to know that it is not by Moses they are to do what he is saying but that it was the God of Israel that was speaking through Moses.

There will be people that will not receive you speaking what God says for you to say. But that is not your concern for if it is God's word and he said to say it, God said that His word would not come back to him void and it will accomplish what it is sent out to do. (**Isaiah 55:11**)

Release the doubt. God already knows the type of enemy he is sending you up against. But just know that God has already prepared you with what is needed to defeat the enemy. God will use what you already have all you are to do is trust God enough to release it. Moses had a rod. David had a sling shot. What has God given you that you have in your possession that you know that the enemy is afraid of. Know that the power of God lies in your ability to trust God with whatever he has given you. Remember you are doing it all for his glory. Stop making excuses………

CHAPTER 2

Release The Doubt

D O YOU REALLY THINK THAT GOD WOULD PUT YOU IN A position that would cause Him to look as though he doesn't know what He is doing? First, of all, you had to have had an experience with God for you to be able to testify of Him.

Here Moses was worried about whether or not the people would believe that he had been with the God of their fathers the God of Abraham, Isaac, and Jacob.

God then showed Moses who He is and the power God had by turning the hand he placed in his chest to become as a leper. Hey, did you catch that. God showed Moses the power God had over flesh. There is also something else we need to know. Just as God showed Moses the power God had over flesh, he also said that He would harden Pharaohs heart to refuse what Moses would ask him to do. (**Exodus 3:19, 20**) Now that may seem to be a bit cruel but how else would the Egyptians as well as the Israelites know that Moses was really sent by the only True and Living God. Yes, I hear you talking, what does that have to do with being a leader? Well ask yourself where am I leading the people to and why? By your experience of deliverance and healing and whatever else God has done in your life. Your testimony is not based on how fantastic you are or how eloquent you speak or even the type of house you live in or car you drive or even the degrees of education you have but to prove to the people what the God you serve can do.

With all that God had showed Moses of what He would be able to do for him Moses still had the mindset that he was not able to do what God was calling him to do. This did not sit well with God because He then got angry at Moses. (**Exodus4:14**) God could not get Moses to take his eyes off his frailty and faults and focus on the power of the Almighty God.

Moses was stuck so God allowed Aaron to be the mouthpiece. Do you truly want someone else to do for God what He wants you to do for Him?

Let me let you in on a little secret. If you really want to tic God off, don't trust and believe him for what He says He will do, that is something that really gets to Him. That was why some of the children of Israel were never able to enter the promise land because of their unbelief in Him. (**Numbers 14:26-38**)

So many times, when people have come unto the Lord, they begin to complain about how bad things are now that they are living for God. They say things like I was doing better before I started serving God or coming to church. Well what they don't realize is that they belonged to the enemy and now they are no longer serving him he's taking back what is his.

Let me explain it to you this way. You go to school to be a plumber so now you have the tools of your trade, in order for you to do what you went to school for. But the company you worked for no longer needs your service so now you go back to school to learn another skill you are now an electrician. So, now in order for you to do the trade of an electrician you need to have the tools of that trade. You cannot use plumber's tools to do an electrician's job. Well that same logic applies to the life that we now live unto the Lord. We are no longer employed by the devil. We work for the Lord now so we cannot use the ways and tools given to us of the devil to build that which is of God and that is why people say what they say when they first come to the Lord they have no knowledge of this concept.

But that is not the only reason. Test. To see that what you said you really meant wanting to be saved and belong to the Kingdom of God. Whether you are serving or will serve God based on what you have or knowing He has you.

Here Pharaoh had taken away the straw that was essential in the making of the bricks which was one of the burdens given to the children of Israel. The Israelites had to get the straw themselves. (**Exodus 5:7**) Some things take place in our life for us to seek the face of God for ourselves.

There was a time in the beginning of my walk with the Lord. I was at home and the Lord suggested to me to cut the grass at my home to give my husband a break because he was working so hard. So, during this time the tradition I was taught was that women were not to wear clothing resembling a man, so I was not wearing pants. I then began to have a conversation with the Lord. I asked him, how would I mow the grass riding on the mower with a skirt? His suggestion was that I could put on a pair of my husband's sweatpants. Well the first thing I said was what would my husband say? I didn't get an answer. So, I did what He told me to do and I got a pair of sweatpants and boy did they feel good. I went out and mowed the grass and when I went to take the pants off the Lord told me to leave them on again the question, what will my husband say? But instead of the Lord giving me what his answer would be He said to me, "How can you preach about being free and be bound?" Well let me tell you I left the pants on and when my husband came home, I told him all about the conversation I had with the Lord and his response was that the Lord did not tell me that. But from that day to this I wear pants. Glory be to God! Whom the Son sets free is free indeed. My suggestion to you today is get over yourself by not worrying about what people will say or think. **RELEASE THE DOUBT!**

CHAPTER 3

Seeing What God Says

G OD SPOKE TO MOSES CONCERNING WHAT HE WOULD DO TO the Egyptians because of the heart of Pharaoh not wanting to let the people of Israel go. The river and everything that contained water turning to blood, to the frogs, to the lice, to the flies, to the pestilence, to the boils, to the hail, to the locusts, to the darkness, and the death of the first born. (**Exodus 7-11**)

Everything that God spoke to Moses he did. Moses and Aaron saw it done. Just ask yourself what of Gods' word do I want to see come to pass. To be the witness of what God said. Let us not get it twisted when God speaks a word it applies to everyone and anyone. With the last thing God spoke about the death of the first born God gave instructions to the children of Israel to get a lamb for the number of people in the home and to roast it whole not boil it and to make bread without yeast in it and bitter herbs and whatever was left to burn it and take the blood of the lamb and place it on the outsides of the door. God's word had gone out and it was going to establish just what He said. If there would be any of the Israelites that did not obey what was told they would have received the same consequences as the Egyptians. (**Exodus 12**)

When we obey God as the children of Israel did. God will be with you at all times. As a pillar of cloud during the day, and a pillar of fire during the night. At all times the glory of the Lord was with them in their obedience to Him.

In this life that we live unto the Lord things are not going to turn out or take place the way we think they should. Our only concern is that God said it and that settles it. It's all up to God on how He is going to do what He does.

From the Israelites point of view the Egyptians were going to retaliate based on everything that happen to them and now the Israelites were out in the wilderness with nothing to defend them, so they thought. Moses had to tell them do not speak out loud concerning what your eyes see but remember what God said He would be and do for you. There are times if we are not careful, we will speak out loud what we see instead of what we believe and trust God for. Moses told them don't worry about what you see God is going to fight this battle for you just hold your peace (keep your mouth closed). (**Exodus 14:12-14**)

Don't you know that the enemy knows when the hand of the Lord is upon your life and when you are sold out unto the Lord that even when the wind blows and the rain comes your soul is still anchored in the Lord? The enemies job is to get you to speak against the God you say you are serving, loving and living for. To get you to speak doubt and unbelief so that what God said he would do gets cancelled out by what you say. Remember Job and how he tried to get him to curse God. (**Job 2:9**) Not only did Job not curse God but he blessed those that tried to get him to doubt, but God spoke to Job not to hold it against them and to pray for them and in his obedience God restored a double portion to him but that's another book maybe. (**Job 41:8-10**)

CHAPTER 4

All Praises Belong To God

GOD DID JUST WHAT HE SAID HE WOULD DO. AND THAT IS WHY all glory and praises belong to Him and Him alone. Nobody can do you like Him. Here the children of Israel saw firsthand the mighty hand of God as well as his word coming to pass right before their eyes. If we could just remember the hand of God over our lives with all the situations and circumstances we found ourselves in whether of our on doing or the enemies traps or the plans of God which ever it maybe just know that if it had not been for the Lord on our side there would have been places we may not have wanted to see ourselves in. That is why we are to give him the praise.

I challenge you to just out of the blue think of a place that God made a way for you. Not waiting when you are up against a test, trial or situation, but just think of how wonderful He has been to you, your family, and to others. Now seeing the hand of God it should always encourage our heart to continue to do more, and more to press the hand of God to do just what he said he was able to do exceeding abundantly above all that we ask or think ....(**Ephesians 3:20**)

The reason we are to keep in remembrance the things God has done is because just like the children of Israel when they found an area that they wanted something to happen at the time they wanted it to happen and it didn't they began to complain. Here they were in the wilderness without any water they could drink and the first thing they did was to complain to Moses. There will always be those who will kick against the prick. But God will deal with them. Just keep yourself humble before the Lord that he may exalt you in due season.

CHAPTER 5

Let God Be God

W HEN THE PEOPLE BEGIN TO COMPLAIN, IT IS NOT FOR YOU to take matters into your own hands. Moses went to God when the people began to murmur against him. (**Exodus 15:24, 25**) And God then gave him the remedy for the situation. These are Gods people just as back in the day of Moses. He knows what is best for them just ask God.

Moses told the people what God had spoken to him. So, when things did not come out right the people had no one to blame but themselves because they knew they had not obeyed the voice of God.

I gave this parable to the congregation that the Lord revealed to me. When you receive your electric bill from the mail carrier do you tell him or her that you are not going to pay it? Why would you? He or she has nothing to do with it they just deliver it. So, if you decide not to pay it does it effect the mail carrier? No, only you are in the dark? But just remember even the mail carrier receives an electric bill. So why did I tell you this? It was just to let you know, let the people know that you are not exempt to the same words that you are delivering to them and if you are subject to obey the voice of God so are they, if they want to receive what God has for them.

Moses was no different from any of the other men. God just decided to use him, and it was up to Moses, whether, or not he would follow what God wanted to do with him.

There will be people who will look at you and say who do they think they are? They are no better than me and they will be right but that has nothing to do with who God wants to use and that is the difference between people who call themselves and God calling them. Even God says you have not chosen me, but I have chosen you. (**John 15:16**)

CHAPTER 6

No One Is An Island

THERE WILL COME A TIME WHEN ALL THAT GOD IS CALLING you to do will become so much larger than you. And before that time comes you should be grooming people getting them to the place of maturity with the talents and anointing God has place in them that He will begin to show you where God can use them in the ministry that the edifying of the saints will take place. Their fruit will then become more fruit as well as much fruit. Then they too will begin to mentor someone for their position as God gives increase and promotion all around.

Well that is the lesson that Moses' father-in-law expressed to him. Instructing him that with all those people there was no way Moses would be able to counsel them all. (**Exodus 18:17-26**)

The assignment is not for you to complete. It is an avenue that

God has given you to steer the people He has given you in the right directions. In letting everyone do their part in the Kingdom everyone arrives at the same destination being a blessing here on earth and making HEAVEN their home.

CHAPTER 7

Spending Time With God

N O ONE KNOWS THE PLANS OF GOD BUT HIS SPIRIT. (ROMANS
8:27) So it is best that we spend time with God for the
spirit of God in us can hear the will of God and his desire can be
done on earth as it is in Heaven. (**Luke 11:2**)

Just think of this. Would you take the directions from a person
who has not been where you are going? My point exactly! God is
the only one that knows where we are going. And if you are not
petitioning God for direction for his people it will be just going
to the building performing some sort of religious act with all
the bells and whistles but really it would be the blind leading the
blind and everyone is going into the ditch.

In being in the presence of God He will begin to speak to you
about you. That's right **"YOU".** So, when God begins to speak
to you about the people in places that they may be struggling in.

Places where there are strongholds and to warn them from the enemy as well as the wrath of God. You can look back and say, "Hey that's not too hard for God look what he has done for me".

Yes, I know we live in the grace of God but if we do not bring to the persons attention that what they are doing God sees it. Because they feel that if none of the church people know it doesn't matter but that is a lie from the pit of hell. The devil just wants them to stay where they are until what they are doing becomes natural, they no longer see it as sin. And there will be times when they will not listen to sound doctrine and you will have to do as Moses and intercede on their behalf and pray that the scales fall from their eyes that they will be able to see the truth. (**Exodus 32:9-14**)

CHAPTER 8

You Are Not God

NOW UP TO THIS POINT GOD HAS ONLY SPOKEN TO YOU ABOUT the way of the people. It is something altogether to see it with your own eyes. So let this not place you where Moses was when he had gotten God not to destroy the people right then but when you see them for yourself you have discredited your witness of the gracious and merciful God by getting in your flesh and telling the person exactly how you feel about what they are doing. (**Exodus 32:19-28**) Oops, there went the chance to love on them. (**Proverbs 10:12, 1 Corinthians 13:4-7**)

Our words of judgment and condemnation can kill a persons' spirit. Let us not resort to allowing the enemy to use us to get more souls for him. There is a character of God besides love that we are to exhibit and that is his mercy for it is the one that God says would come back to us. (**Matthew 5:7**)

Long story short. Do not allow the people to exalt or to complain so much to you that you begin to take matters into your own hands for they will also be the same ones that will cause you to get on the wrong side of God.

Here the children of Israel began to murmur and complain again about what they didn't have as a convenience. Instead of them asking Moses to pray to God about what to do about them not having any water they complained to Moses. So, Moses did what he knew to do and went to God. God gave him instructions in how to get the water. But Moses did not have mercy upon the people and was angry and in his anger, he did not do what God instructed him to do. He did what his flesh called for him to do and that is why we are to always remember we are not God. (**Numbers 20:1-12**)

It cost Moses not to finish what he started out to do taking the people into the promise land.

This is a lesson well learned. Stay on the track of being obedient to the voice of God that you will be able to see the fruits of your labor in seeing the people God has placed in your life, receive salvation, be delivered, made whole, as well as prosper as their soul prospers. For that is what our mission is to get the people to receive the promises of God.

Remember you are not the one to take them there. God is to take them there through you for He is the way the truth and the life. For no one can get there except by HIS WORD. (**John 14:6**)

CONCLUSION

This is really, quite simply. If God is not calling you to lead people don't. The day of judgment is coming, and you are going to talk about all the things you did in the Lords name. But the answer that comes will not be the one you will want to hear...... I never knew you: depart from me, ye that work iniquity. (**Matthew 7:22, 23**) You see you could have done all that you said you did, but did God call you to do it. All you did was out of your own desires (flesh). That is what God calls iniquity. Do what you are called to do and do no more. You don't get brownie points for doing extra. We are only going to get paid for what God has already predestinated us to do if we do it.

We need to start what has been finished, so that we can finish what was started. Preaching the gospel to a lost and dying world, and reconciling man back to God. Releasing people from the condemnation that they are not good enough for God to love them because of their past or even where they are right now.

But teach them that they do not have to do something good for God to love them. He already does. We are to introduce them to the love of the Father by living out the love of the Father we have received. For God so loved the world he gave.......This is my commandment. That ye love one another, as I have loved you. (**John 3:16; 15:12**) Isn't that what Jesus did. He started and he finished it. He just wants us to continue doing it so that we can be as Paul and say I have fought a good fight, I have finished the race, I have kept the faith........... (**2 Timothy 4:6-8**)

Well done, good and faithful servant.... (**Matthew 25:21**) Isn't that what you want to hear I know I do.

Printed in the United States
By Bookmasters